Dad, Share Your Life With Me

Dad, Share Your Life With Me

A Thoughtful Guided Journal
to Capture Your Father's Memories,
Wisdom and Life Lessons
for Future Generations

Aria Capri Publishing

The original purchaser of this book has permission to reproduce the pages of this book for personal use only. No other parts of this publication may be reproduced in whole or in part, shared with others, stored in a retrieval system, digitized, or transmitted in any form without written permission from the publisher.

Copyright 2021, Aria Capri Publishing Group (Aria Capri International Inc). All rights reserved.

Authors:
Aria Capri Publishing Group
Mauricio Vasquez

First Printing: April 2025

ISBN 978-1-998729-22-7 (Electronic book)
ISBN 978-1-998729-21-0 (Hardcover book)
ISBN 978-1-998729-20-3 (Paperback)

Dear Valued Customer,

As a family-owned business, your review means the world to us.

It only takes a moment—just scan the QR code to leave your feedback. Your review helps others discover this book and create more love and connection in their own families.

Thank you for your support!

Mauricio

Want to Capture Mom's Story Too?

Celebrate your mother's life and legacy with the companion journal, Mom, Share Your Live with Me.

Scan the QR code to get your copy and preserve her memories for generations to come.

Because both stories deserve to be told. 🖤

Empower Your Connections:
Discover More Tools to Strengthen Relationships.
Scan the QR Code Today

  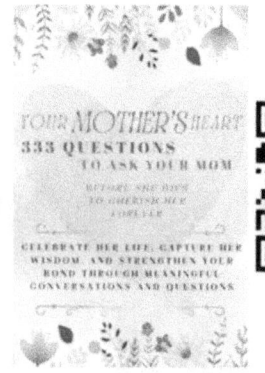 

Table of Contents

INTRODUCTION 1

MAKING THIS JOURNAL YOUR OWN 2

ABOUT ME & KEEPSAKES OF MY TIME 4

MY EARLIEST MEMORIES 7

MY CHILDHOOD YEARS 14

HOW I SPENT MY TIME 29

MY PEOPLE 36

MY LIFE THROUGH THE PEOPLE I'VE KNOWN 40

THE HEART OF FATHERHOOD 64

MY GUIDING PRINCIPLES 72

PAGES OF WISDOM 78

QUICK QUESTIONS FROM MY LIFE 92

WORDS FOR THE ONES I LOVE 110

Introduction

This journal was created for you—fathers of all types, both biological and those who stepped into the role—to capture the important moments that have shaped your life.

Your stories and wisdom can only be passed down to future generations if you take the time to share them.

This book is designed to help you write down your memories, stories, and thoughts, turning this guided journal into a precious keepsake to share with your children, loved ones, and future generations.

The thoughtful questions make it easy to record everything from your childhood memories and important life lessons to your hopes for the future.

When completed, this book will help your children and grandchildren better understand your family's history and roots.

Most importantly, this journal will tell your unique story. It's how your family will learn about who you really are, beyond just being "Dad," and will create a meaningful connection with them. This lasting keepsake gives you the chance to inspire future generations with your experiences, accomplishments, and the wisdom you've gained throughout your life.

Making This Journal Your Own

This journal is your personal space for reflection—there's no rulebook to follow.

Make this experience work for you. Jump between questions that catch your interest, circle back to others when memories surface, or methodically work from page to page. The path you take is entirely yours to choose.

Every question is simply an invitation. Some might spark detailed stories, while others might not connect with your experience at all. Feel free to change a question to better match your journey.

The most valuable entries often come when you let your thoughts flow naturally. Don't worry about crafting perfect sentences or organizing your thoughts;—just let your authentic memories and feelings guide your pen. Your family will treasure your genuine voice more than polished prose.

Bring your stories to life with vivid details. Rather than writing "we went to the beach," specify "we built sandcastles at Lighthouse Point on that sweltering July afternoon in 1982." Instead of "I drove my first car," share how "my hands trembled with excitement on the wheel of that rusted blue Ford Mustang with the cracked leather seats." These specifics transform memories into experiences your readers can almost see and feel.

This journey through your memories deserves time and space. Consider setting aside a regular moment—perhaps Sunday mornings with coffee or quiet weekday evenings—to revisit and record your stories. Many fathers find it takes several months to complete their journal, allowing memories to unfold naturally.

For a different approach, consider having someone interview you. A child or grandchild might enjoy asking these questions while recording your spoken responses, capturing your voice, laughter, and the natural rhythm of conversation.

The notes pages at the end of each section offer extra room when memories overflow, space for photos that complement your stories, or spots to answer additional questions from our website.

Remember—this process isn't about creating a perfect document, but about sharing the unique story that only you can tell. Enjoy the journey of rediscovery as you create this lasting gift for your family.

To enrich your journaling journey, we've created a special bonus: a 30-Day Family Bonding Challenge filled with simple, meaningful activities to enjoy with your loved ones.

Scan the QR code to download your free printable and create even more memories—together.

About Me & Keepsakes of My Time

About Me

MY FULL NAME	
BIRTHDAY	
BIRTHPLACE	EYE COLOR
HEIGHT	HAIR COLOR
ANY SPECIAL TRAITS	

ATTACH YOUR PHOTO HERE:

A Snapshot of My Time

TODAY'S DATE:

POPULATION OF MY CITY:	POPULATION OF MY COUNTRY:
PRESIDENT OR PRIME MINISTER OF MY COUNTRY:	WORLD POPULATION:

COMMON COSTS AT THIS MOMENT IN TIME:

A TANK OF GAS:	A BASIC CAR WASH:
A CUP OF COFFEE:	A 6-PACK OF BEER OR SOFT DRINKS:
A FAMILY MEAL:	A MOVIE TICKET:
A PAIR OF WORK OR RUNNING SHOES:	A HAIRCUT:
POSTAGE STAMP	MONTHLY RENT/ MORTGAGE PAYMENT
A TOOL OR HARDWARE ITEM I USE:	A BASIC SMARTPHONE OR MOBILE PLAN:

ADD A HEADLINE OR FRONT PAGE FROM
TODAY'S NEWS TO CAPTURE THE WORLD AROUND YOU:

My Earliest Memories

Is there a special story behind your name or were you named in honor of someone important to your family?

_____
_____
_____
_____
_____
_____

How has your relationship with your name changed throughout your life? Were there times you wished for a different name?

_____
_____
_____
_____
_____
_____

If you could have chosen your own name at any point in your life, what would you have picked and why?

_____
_____
_____
_____
_____
_____

What stage of life were your parents in when you arrived? How do you think their ages shaped how they raised you?

_____
_____
_____
_____
_____
_____

What stories have been passed down about the day you entered the world? Were there any unusual circumstances or memorable moments surrounding your birth?"

_____
_____
_____
_____
_____
_____

How did your early health shape your childhood? Were there any significant health challenges or were you particularly robust as a baby?

_____
_____
_____
_____
_____
_____

What childhood anecdotes did your parents love to retell about your baby years? Which stories seemed to bring them the most joy or amusement?

_____
_____
_____
_____
_____
_____

What moment from your early childhood stands out as your first clear memory? What emotions or sensations do you still recall from that experience?

_____
_____
_____
_____
_____
_____

How did your upbringing as a baby differ from your parents' experiences? What parenting traditions did your family maintain across generations, and which ones did they consciously change?

_____
_____
_____
_____
_____
_____

What details can you recall or have you been told about your very first home? How did that space shape your earliest days, and what memories or stories are connected to it?

_____
_____
_____
_____
_____
_____

Which aspects of your personality do you recognize as echoes of your mother and father? How have these inherited traits influenced your own journey through life?

_____
_____
_____
_____
_____
_____

Notes

Notes

My Childhood Years

What treasured childhood possessions held special meaning for you? How did these cherished items come into your life, and what memories do they still evoke?

_____
_____
_____
_____
_____
_____

Which games captured your imagination as a child? How did your play differ when you were with friends versus those quiet moments of solitary imagination?

_____
_____
_____
_____
_____
_____

What shadows or worries populated your childhood imagination? How did you navigate these fears, and did any adults help you overcome them?

_____
_____
_____
_____
_____
_____

Which sensory experiences immediately transport you back to your childhood days? What memories and emotions surface when you encounter these echoes from your past?

___

Which spaces served as the backdrop for your childhood adventures? How did these special places shape your experiences and foster your sense of freedom or security?

___

What was your personal space like during your growing years? How did having your own room—or sharing with others—influence your sense of identity?

___

How did your childhood neighborhood shape who you became? What aspects of your community did you treasure, and which elements did you wish were different?

_____
_____
_____
_____
_____
_____

How did your family gather around food during your childhood years? What unspoken rules or cherished traditions defined these daily rituals?

_____
_____
_____
_____
_____
_____

How did your childhood kitchen engage all your senses? What aromas, flavors, sounds, and visual memories still linger from this central space in your early life?

_____
_____
_____
_____
_____
_____

Which foods triggered your childhood aversions, and how has your relationship with these tastes evolved over the decades? What stories surround your food preferences?

_____
_____
_____
_____
_____

What responsibilities were entrusted to you in your childhood home? How did these early duties shape your character, and what emotions do you associate with them now?

_____
_____
_____
_____
_____
_____

Beyond your parents, which adults illuminated your path during childhood? How did these significant figures influence who you would become, and what wisdom did they impart?

_____
_____
_____
_____
_____
_____

Which shared activities created bonds between you and your parents? What sensations and emotions resurface when you recall these moments of connection, whether with one parent or both?

_____
_____
_____
_____
_____
_____

How did the dynamics of your relationships with each parent differ during your formative years? What circumstances or personality traits influenced these connections, and how have they evolved?

_____
_____
_____
_____
_____
_____

What challenges tested your family's resilience during your childhood? How were you either protected from or included in navigating these difficulties, and what lessons emerged from these experiences?

_____
_____
_____
_____
_____
_____

How were you first introduced to managing money as a child? What memories do you have of receiving allowance, and which treasures or experiences did you save for?"

How did your family's financial situation shape your childhood understanding of money? What lessons about abundance or scarcity did you absorb during those formative years?

What strategies did you develop to navigate the social currents of your youth? How did you balance your own values against the desires to belong or fit in with your peers?

Which words from your teachers have remained with you through the decades? How did their assessments of your academic performance or behavior influence your self-perception?

_____
_____
_____
_____
_____

Which knowledge or skills do you wish had been part of your formal education? How might your path have differed if these subjects had been available to you as a student?

_____
_____
_____
_____
_____
_____

Which areas of learning captured your imagination or sparked your curiosity during your school years? How did these academic interests shape your developing sense of self?

_____
_____
_____
_____
_____

Beyond the classroom, which activities enriched your school experience? How did these pursuits—whether athletic, musical, or otherwise—contribute to your growth and identity?

_____
_____
_____
_____
_____

Which teams or athletes inspired your loyalty and excitement during childhood? What memories do you have of celebrating victories or commiserating defeats alongside fellow fans?

_____
_____
_____
_____
_____

Which moments from your high school experience have remained vivid across the decades? What emotions resurface when you revisit these formative scenes from your teenage years?

_____
_____
_____
_____
_____

What accomplishment from your youth still brings a sense of pride when you reflect upon it? How did this achievement shape your confidence or influence your path forward?

_____
_____
_____
_____
_____
_____

How did freedom feel during those childhood summers away from school? Which seasonal rituals or adventures defined your experiences of those seemingly endless days?

_____
_____
_____
_____
_____
_____

Which friendships formed the emotional cornerstone of your youth? How have these significant relationships evolved over time, and which connections have endured through the decades?

_____
_____
_____
_____
_____
_____

Which companions in your youth challenged your parents' expectations or concerns? How did you navigate the tension between your own social choices and your parents' protective instincts?

_____
_____
_____
_____
_____
_____

How did your family address boundaries and consequences during your childhood? What strategies did you develop for managing those moments when you found yourself at odds with parental authority?

_____
_____
_____
_____
_____
_____

How did these travels beyond your everyday world shape your understanding of both family bonds and the wider world?

_____
_____
_____
_____
_____
_____

Which annual celebrations marked the rhythm of your family's year together? What traditions, preparations, and moments of connection defined these special occasions for you?

_____
_____
_____
_____
_____
_____

Which celebration from your childhood has remained especially vivid in your memory? What made this particular occasion transcend the ordinary and become part of your lasting narrative?

_____
_____
_____
_____
_____
_____

How would you characterize the emotional landscape of your childhood years? Which elements brought joy or challenge, and how have these experiences influenced your understanding of happiness?

_____
_____
_____
_____
_____
_____

If you could whisper wisdom across time to your younger self, what insights would you share? Which understandings have you gained that might have eased or enriched your teenage journey?

___
___
___
___
___
___
___
___
___
___
___

Notes

Notes

How I Spent My Time

How did your life's professional path take shape over time? Which influences, mentors, or pivotal moments guided your career choices, and in what ways did serendipity play a role in your journey?

What educational or service path did you pursue after your school years? How did these formative experiences beyond the classroom expand your horizons or shape your skills and values?

Which moments from your early adult years stand as touchstones in your memory? What discoveries, relationships, or achievements from this time of transition continue to resonate with you today?

When you reflect on the roads taken and not taken after high school, which choices invite reconsideration? What wisdom have you gained about paths chosen or opportunities missed during these formative years?

_____
_____
_____
_____
_____

What insights about learning pathways and personal development would you want to share with your grandchildren and beyond? Which enduring principles about education or service transcend the changing landscapes of opportunity?

_____
_____
_____
_____
_____

Which position marked your entry into the world of earning? How did that first experience of exchange—your time and effort for compensation—shape your understanding of work and value?

_____
_____
_____
_____
_____

What path led you to your first employment opportunity? Which combination of circumstances, connections, or personal initiative opened this initial door to the working world?

How has your professional journey unfolded across the decades? Which positions served as stepping stones, which as detours, and which unexpectedly transformed your path?

Which professional role brought you the greatest sense of fulfillment or joy? What elements of this position—the people, purpose, or possibilities—resonated most deeply with your values and strengths?

Which space became your first independent domain after leaving your childhood home? How did this transition and your chosen companions (or solitude) shape your emerging adult identity?

_____
_____
_____
_____
_____

Which lesson acquired during your education has proven most enduringly valuable beyond classroom walls? How has this knowledge or skill served as a foundation throughout your life's various chapters?

_____
_____
_____
_____
_____
_____

Who guided you through the rite of passage toward driving independence? What memories or lessons from those teaching moments have stayed with you throughout your years behind the wheel?

_____
_____
_____
_____
_____

Which animal companions have shared your journey through the years? How did these beloved creatures touch your heart, and which moments with them have remained most vivid in your memory?

_____
_____
_____
_____
_____
_____

Which pursuits have captured your passion and interest beyond your working life? How did these meaningful activities first enter your world, and how have they evolved alongside you through different life stages?

_____
_____
_____
_____
_____
_____

Which experiences consistently awaken your sense of delight or fulfillment? How do these cherished activities connect you to your authentic self or to what matters most in your life?

_____
_____
_____
_____
_____
_____

Notes

My People

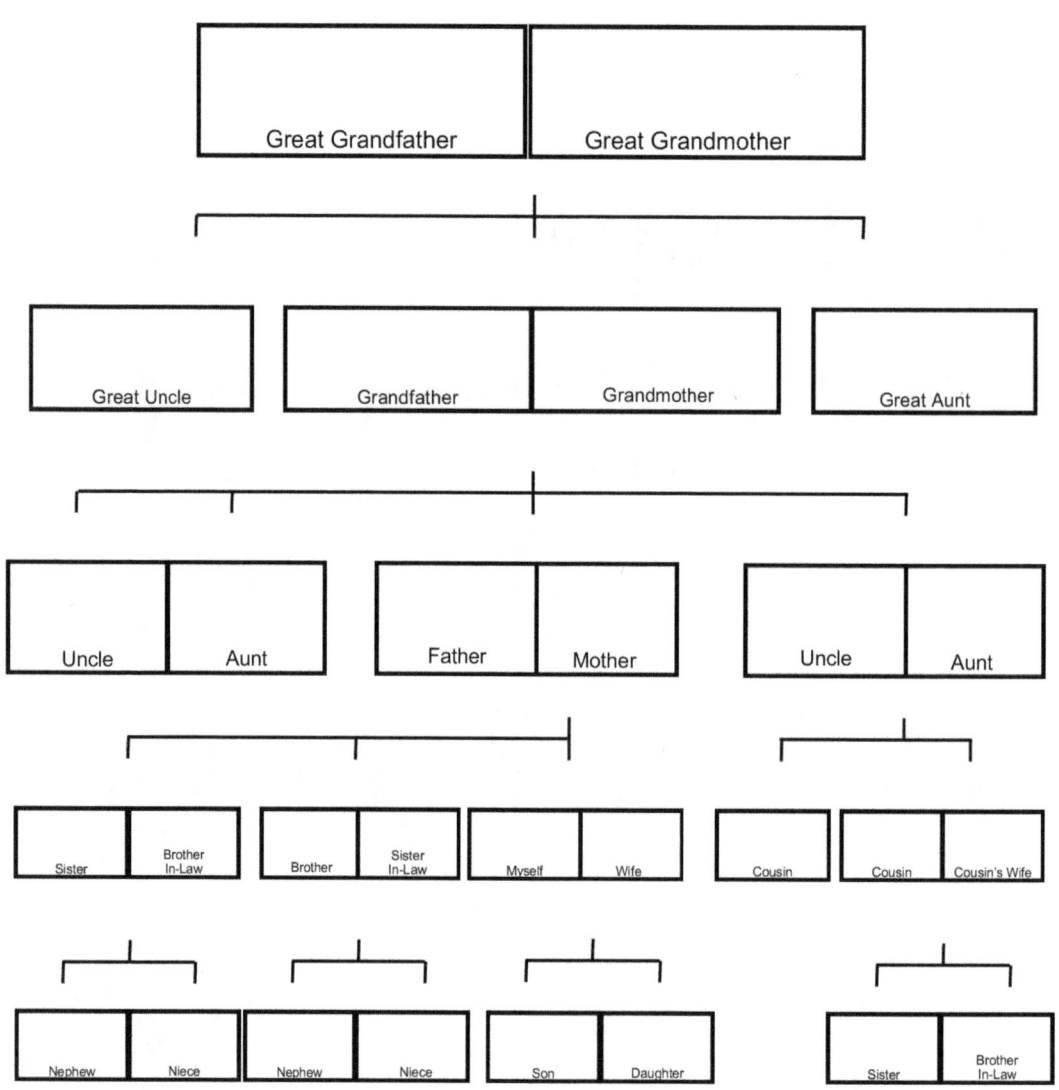

37 MY PEOPLE

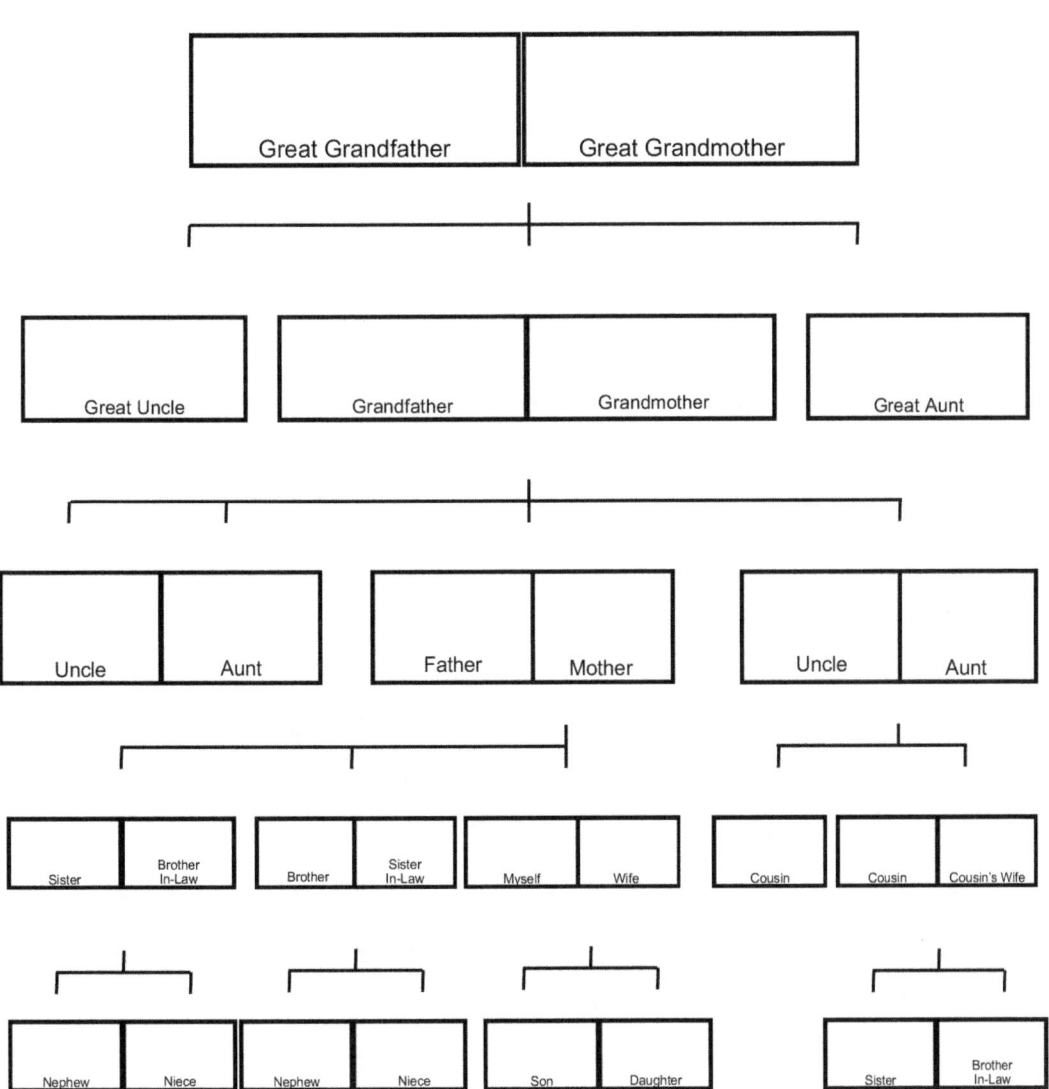

38 MY PEOPLE

Notes

My Life Through the People I've Known

About My Parents

FIRST NAME

FAMILY NAME

BIRTH PLACE	DATE OF BIRTH
EYE COLOR	HAIR COLOR

OCCUPATION

FIRST NAME

FAMILY NAME

BIRTH PLACE	DATE OF BIRTH
EYE COLOR	HAIR COLOR

OCCUPATION

How did the unique dynamics between you and each of your parents shape your formative years? In what ways have these foundational relationships evolved as you transitioned from child to adult, and what insights have you gained through this evolution?

Which essential lessons or values did you inherit from each parent's distinct influence? How have these specific gifts—whether skills, perspectives, or appreciations—continued to resonate throughout your life journey?

My Brothers and/or Sisters

FIRST NAME

FAMILY NAME

BIRTH PLACE	DATE OF BIRTH
EYE COLOR	HAIR COLOR

OCCUPATION

FIRST NAME

FAMILY NAME

BIRTH PLACE	DATE OF BIRTH
EYE COLOR	HAIR COLOR

OCCUPATION

FIRST NAME

FAMILY NAME

BIRTH PLACE	DATE OF BIRTH
EYE COLOR	HAIR COLOR

OCCUPATION

FIRST NAME

FAMILY NAME

BIRTH PLACE	DATE OF BIRTH
EYE COLOR	HAIR COLOR

OCCUPATION

How do familial echoes appear between you and your siblings, whether in appearance, temperament, or perspective? Which shared inheritances connect you, and which distinct qualities have defined your separate paths?

What characterized the emotional landscape between you and your siblings during childhood? How did these early relational dynamics shape both your shared experiences and individual development?

_____
_____
_____
_____
_____
_____
_____
_____
_____

How has the tapestry of your sibling relationships evolved through life's different seasons? Which transformative experiences or understandings have deepened or redirected these fundamental connections as you've grown together?

_____
_____
_____
_____
_____
_____
_____
_____
_____
_____

About my Grandparents

FIRST NAME

FAMILY NAME

BIRTH PLACE | DATE OF BIRTH

EYE COLOR | HAIR COLOR

OCCUPATION

FIRST NAME

FAMILY NAME

BIRTH PLACE | DATE OF BIRTH

EYE COLOR | HAIR COLOR

OCCUPATION

FIRST NAME

FAMILY NAME

BIRTH PLACE | DATE OF BIRTH

EYE COLOR | HAIR COLOR

OCCUPATION

FIRST NAME

FAMILY NAME

BIRTH PLACE | DATE OF BIRTH

EYE COLOR | HAIR COLOR

OCCUPATION

How did the rhythms of personality and character flow across the generations of your family? Which traits seemed to skip generations or transform as they passed from your grandparents to your parents to you?

What emotional distances or intimacies characterized your relationships with your grandparents? Which moments with them have crystallized into stories that still carry meaning or resonance through the years?

Which wisdom from your grandparents has served as a compass point in your journey? How have their lived experiences or explicit teachings continued to guide your path long after the conversations ended?

My Kids

FIRST NAME

FAMILY NAME

BIRTH PLACE	DATE OF BIRTH
EYE COLOR	HAIR COLOR

OCCUPATION

FIRST NAME

FAMILY NAME

BIRTH PLACE	DATE OF BIRTH
EYE COLOR	HAIR COLOR

OCCUPATION

FIRST NAME

FAMILY NAME

BIRTH PLACE	DATE OF BIRTH
EYE COLOR	HAIR COLOR

OCCUPATION

FIRST NAME

FAMILY NAME

BIRTH PLACE	DATE OF BIRTH
EYE COLOR	HAIR COLOR

OCCUPATION

What unique qualities in each of your children continue to inspire your admiration and pride? How have these distinctive strengths revealed themselves over time, and which moments have most powerfully illustrated their special gifts?

What hopes do you hold in your heart for the generations that follow you? Beyond material success, which values, experiences, or forms of fulfillment do you most deeply wish would grace the lives of your children and grandchildren?

Family

Which family members mirror aspects of your own spirit or journey most closely? With whom have you forged the deepest connections, and how have these special relationships evolved through life's changing seasons?

_____
_____
_____
_____
_____
_____
_____
_____
_____
_____

What challenging moments have tested the fabric of your family relationships over time? How did these conflicts reshape your understanding of forgiveness, reconciliation, or the complex dynamics that both challenge and strengthen family bonds?

_____
_____
_____
_____
_____
_____
_____
_____
_____
_____

Which threads of history, legacy, or unusual circumstance are woven into your family's unique tapestry? What stories of notable ancestors, meaningful objects, or distinctive traditions connect you to a heritage larger than your individual experience?

Friends

Which companions have walked most intimately alongside you through life's journey? What moments of connection, adventure, or mutual support with these chosen family members have shaped your understanding of friendship itself?

_____
_____
_____
_____
_____
_____
_____
_____
_____

Which friendship has weathered the longest passage of time in your life? How has this enduring connection evolved through the different chapters you've both navigated, and what has sustained its continuity?

_____
_____
_____
_____
_____
_____
_____
_____
_____

When has the fragility of human connection revealed itself within one of your valued friendships? How did you navigate this landscape of hurt or misunderstanding, and what insights about reconciliation or acceptance emerged from this experience?

_____
_____
_____
_____
_____
_____
_____
_____
_____
_____

Whose wisdom has served as a trusted lighthouse during your moments of uncertainty or decision? Which specific guidance from this trusted advisor proved particularly illuminating, perhaps altering your course in meaningful ways?

_____
_____
_____
_____
_____
_____
_____
_____
_____
_____

When has the fragility of human connection revealed itself within one of your valued friendships? How did you navigate this landscape of hurt or misunderstanding, and what insights about reconciliation or acceptance emerged from this experience?

Whose wisdom has served as a trusted lighthouse during your moments of uncertainty or decision? Which specific guidance from this trusted advisor proved particularly illuminating, perhaps altering your course in meaningful ways?

Relationships

When did you first step into the world of romantic connection through a formal date? How did this inaugural experience unfold, and what emotions or impressions from that milestone occasion have stayed with you?

_____
_____
_____
_____
_____
_____
_____
_____
_____

Which chapters from your heart's journey might offer insights into your romantic history? What early attractions or partings of ways helped shape your understanding of love and its complex terrain?

_____
_____
_____
_____
_____
_____
_____
_____
_____

What confluence of timing, circumstance, or perhaps intention brought you and your life partner together? How did your relationship's beginning foreshadow or contrast with the deeper connection that would develop?

_____
_____
_____
_____
_____
_____
_____
_____
_____
_____

Which aspects of your partner's essence have most profoundly captured your heart over time? How have these cherished qualities revealed themselves in both ordinary moments and extraordinary circumstances?

_____
_____
_____
_____
_____
_____
_____
_____
_____
_____

How did your journey from courtship to marriage unfold in its most significant moments? Which scenes from your proposal and wedding day remain vivid in your memory, becoming touchstones of your shared story?

_____
_____
_____
_____
_____
_____
_____
_____
_____
_____

What wisdom about love and partnership has life revealed to you through experience rather than theory? Which insights about sustaining connection would you most want to preserve in your family's emotional inheritance?

_____
_____
_____
_____
_____
_____
_____
_____
_____
_____

Notes

Notes

The Heart of Fatherhood

When did the reality of impending fatherhood first truly dawn upon you? What complex emotions and thoughts surfaced in that pivotal moment when you recognized your life was about to transform?

___

How did the ripples of your journey into fatherhood spread through your circle of loved ones? Which reactions or responses to your news particularly surprised, touched, or amused you?

___

How did fatherhood rewrite the contours of your identity and daily existence? Which aspects of yourself emerged, evolved, or receded as you stepped into this transformative role?

_____
_____
_____
_____
_____
_____
_____
_____
_____

Which dimensions of being a father tested your capacities or pushed you beyond familiar territories? How did you navigate these challenges, and what did they reveal about your character or values?

_____
_____
_____
_____
_____
_____
_____
_____
_____

How did the lived reality of fatherhood compare with the version you had imagined beforehand? Which assumptions were upended, and which unexpected gifts or challenges appeared along your parenting journey?

_____
_____
_____
_____
_____
_____
_____
_____
_____
_____

In what ways did your own childhood experiences serve as either blueprint or counterpoint as you shaped your parenting approach? How consciously did you embrace or redirect the patterns from your past?

_____
_____
_____
_____
_____
_____
_____
_____
_____
_____

If you could send wisdom across time to your younger self just stepping into fatherhood, which insights or reassurances would you most want to share? What would you want new fathers to understand about the journey ahead?

_____
_____
_____
_____
_____
_____
_____
_____
_____
_____

Through which seasons of fatherhood did you find the greatest joy or resonance with your authentic self? Which phases stretched you beyond your comfort or presented unexpected challenges, and what insights emerged from navigating these different landscapes of parenting?

_____
_____
_____
_____
_____
_____
_____
_____
_____

How has the terrain of childhood shifted between your generation and that of your children or grandchildren? Which evolutions in society do you see as enriching young lives today, and which contemporary challenges would you have wished to shield them from?

Notes

Notes

My Guiding Principles

How did faith or spiritual understanding manifest in your childhood home? Which sacred traditions or perspectives were passed to you, and how have you either embraced, transformed, or reimagined this inheritance throughout your life journey?

_____
_____
_____
_____
_____
_____
_____
_____
_____

Through which spiritual seasons has your soul traveled across the decades? How have your understandings of meaning, transcendence, or connection to something greater shifted through life's various challenges and revelations?

_____
_____
_____
_____
_____
_____
_____
_____
_____

Which aspects of your homeland's character or ideals have most deeply resonated with your own values? How has your relationship with national identity evolved through different chapters of both your life and your country's history?

___

Which experiences, relationships, or awakenings have guided the evolution of your political perspective? How has your understanding of society and governance either remained steadfast or transformed as you've witnessed history unfold?

___

How were the boundaries of masculinity and femininity drawn in your childhood world? What emotions or reflections did these defined roles evoke in your younger self, and how has your perspective on gender evolved through the decades?

How have evolving awarenesses or convictions reshaped your daily choices and practices? Which shifts in your understanding have inspired tangible changes in how you interact with the world around you?

Which causes have you chosen to support with your resources through the years? How do these particular expressions of generosity reflect your deepest values or perhaps connect to significant experiences in your own life story?"

_____
_____
_____
_____
_____
_____
_____
_____
_____
_____

Which principles have served as your north star through life's various chapters and challenges? Which essential truths or approaches to living would you most hope to see echoing through the lives of your children's children and beyond?"

_____
_____
_____
_____
_____
_____
_____
_____
_____
_____

Notes

Pages of Wisdom

If you were to paint a self-portrait through words rather than images, which essential qualities and contradictions would you include? How has your understanding of your own character evolved as you've moved through different chapters of life?

___

Which health patterns or inherited conditions in your lineage might provide important context for future generations? What wisdom about wellbeing would you wish to pass along beyond the genetic information itself?

___

How has your personal definition of a life well-lived evolved through your experiences? Which individuals have embodied your ideals of meaningful achievement, and what qualities in their journeys have particularly resonated with your own values?

_____
_____
_____
_____
_____
_____
_____
_____
_____
_____

Which season of your life has felt most aligned with your authentic self or brought the greatest sense of fulfillment? What was it about this particular time that allowed you to flourish or experience life most deeply?

_____
_____
_____
_____
_____
_____
_____
_____
_____
_____

Whose presence has left the most profound imprint on the landscape of your life journey? How did this pivotal relationship shape your path, your perspective, or your understanding of what matters most?

_____
_____
_____
_____
_____
_____
_____
_____
_____

When you gaze back across the landscape of your years, which paths do you wish you had walked more slowly or explored more fully? Which moments or pursuits deserved more space in the story you've lived?

_____
_____
_____
_____
_____
_____
_____
_____
_____

Which inner fires have fueled your journey through both calm waters and storms? What sources of purpose or passion have consistently rekindled your spirit when challenges or routine threatened to dim your light?

_____
_____
_____
_____
_____
_____
_____
_____
_____
_____

Which wisdom about wealth, resources, and their proper place in a well-lived life would you inscribe in your family's legacy? What financial insights—earned perhaps through both abundance and scarcity—might serve as guideposts for those who follow you?

_____
_____
_____
_____
_____
_____
_____
_____
_____

How has your relationship with place and property shaped your understanding of what makes a home? Which perspectives on dwelling, investment, and rootedness would you offer to those navigating today's different landscape of possibilities?

_____
_____
_____
_____
_____
_____
_____
_____
_____
_____

Beyond the profound work of parenthood, which accomplishment stands as your most meaningful contribution or personal victory? What creation, connection, or conquering of adversity reflects the essence of who you've become?

_____
_____
_____
_____
_____
_____
_____
_____
_____
_____

Which choices or paths not taken still echo with possibility or longing in your heart? How have you made peace with life's inevitable regrets, or what reconciliations do you still hope might lie ahead?

_____
_____
_____
_____
_____
_____
_____
_____
_____
_____

When has life's apparent unraveling revealed itself to be a necessary reweaving of your story? Which moments of disappointment or loss surprisingly opened doors to unexpected growth or joy?

_____
_____
_____
_____
_____
_____
_____
_____
_____
_____

Which hardships or collective struggles from your era would you wish to spare those who follow you? What wisdom from navigating difficult chapters might serve as protection for future generations?

_____
_____
_____
_____
_____
_____
_____
_____
_____

Through which season of profound challenge did your resilience reveal itself most clearly? What inner resources or external supports enabled you to weather this storm, and how did this experience reshape you?

_____
_____
_____
_____
_____
_____
_____
_____
_____

When has fear cast its longest shadow across your path? How did you find your way through this darkness, and what enduring wisdom emerged from facing what once terrified you?

_____
_____
_____
_____
_____
_____
_____
_____
_____

Which experiences have offered such profound awakening or joy that you would prescribe them as essential medicine for the human spirit? What transformative encounters with life would you wish for everyone to know at least once?

_____
_____
_____
_____
_____
_____
_____
_____
_____

Which moments in your journey have filled you with the deepest sense of wonder or awe? What experiences have expanded your understanding of what's possible in this life and continue to inspire you when remembered?"

_____
_____
_____
_____
_____
_____
_____
_____
_____
_____

Which aspect of your character continues to invite growth or transformation, even now? How has your relationship with this particular quality shaped your life's journey and self-understanding?"

_____
_____
_____
_____
_____
_____
_____
_____
_____
_____

Which hidden wisdoms have you discovered about crafting a life of meaning and satisfaction? What principles or practices, perhaps invisible to outside observers, have most consistently guided you toward genuine fulfillment?"

_____
_____
_____
_____
_____
_____
_____
_____
_____

Which words of wisdom, offered perhaps at a pivotal moment or carried quietly through decades, have proven most illuminating on your path? How did this particular guidance transform your choices or perspective when you embraced it?"

_____
_____
_____
_____
_____
_____
_____
_____
_____

Which hidden wisdoms have you discovered about crafting a life of meaning and satisfaction? What principles or practices, perhaps invisible to outside observers, have most consistently guided you toward genuine fulfillment?"

_____
_____
_____
_____
_____
_____
_____
_____
_____
_____

Which words of wisdom, offered perhaps at a pivotal moment or carried quietly through decades, have proven most illuminating on your path? How did this particular guidance transform your choices or perspective when you embraced it?"

_____
_____
_____
_____
_____
_____
_____
_____
_____
_____

If your voice could reach across time to the eyes and hearts of those who will carry your lineage forward, which truths about your essence would you most want to preserve? Beyond facts and dates, what understanding of who you truly were would you hope might echo through the generations yet unborn?

_____
_____
_____
_____
_____
_____
_____
_____
_____
_____

Which wisdom, distilled from your unique journey through joy and challenge, would you offer as lanterns to illuminate the paths of those who follow? What understandings, hard-won through lived experience, might serve as both compass and comfort for fellow travelers on life's road?

_____
_____
_____
_____
_____
_____
_____
_____

Notes

Quick Questions from My Life

Which sound first emerged from your childhood voice as meaningful language? What response did this initial verbal expression evoke from those who witnessed your entry into the world of words?

At what moment in your youth did you first experience the tender connection of a kiss? What emotions or awakenings accompanied this threshold crossing into new emotional territory?

When did your heart first recognize that unique magnetic pull we call love? How did this inaugural experience of profound connection reshape your understanding of yourself and others?

Which cinematic experience first transported you into the collective magic of a darkened theater? How did this initial encounter with storytelling on the big screen impact your young imagination?

When did you first encounter the adult ritual of alcohol consumption? What circumstances surrounded this initiation, and what impressions did it leave upon you?

When did you first take command of a vehicle, experiencing that simultaneous freedom and responsibility? What feelings accompanied your hands on the wheel during those initial moments of driving independence?

Which vehicle first belonged truly to you, becoming both symbol and tool of your emerging autonomy? What relationship did you develop with this mechanical companion, and did you christen it with a name that reflected its character or meaning in your life?

___

Which musical recording did you first select and purchase as an expression of your own taste? How did this initial investment in sound reflect your emerging identity or emotional landscape?

___

Which destination marked your first journey beyond family oversight? How did this initial taste of independent travel shape your sense of self or expand your view of the world?

_____
_____
_____
_____
_____
_____
_____
_____
_____

Which doorway did you first walk through seeking formal employment? What hopes, anxieties, or aspirations accompanied you as you presented yourself to potential employers for the first time?

_____
_____
_____
_____
_____
_____
_____
_____
_____

For whom did you first prepare food as an act of hospitality or care beyond family obligations? What emotions or intentions infused this initial sharing of nourishment with someone from your chosen circle?

_____
_____
_____
_____
_____
_____
_____
_____
_____

Where did your vehicle first bear the marks of the imperfect human navigation of roads? How did you respond to this initial encounter with automotive vulnerability or limitation?

_____
_____
_____
_____
_____
_____
_____
_____
_____

Which journey first lifted you above the clouds, changing your perspective on distance and possibility? What sensations or revelations accompanied your initial experience of flight?

Which foreign soil first received your footsteps beyond your homeland's borders? How did this initial international encounter reshape your understanding of culture, place, or your own identity?

My Favorite Fives

Which destinations have left the most indelible impressions upon your soul? Which landscapes, cities, or sacred spaces continue to inhabit your dreams and memories long after your physical departure?"

1. _____
2. _____
3. _____
4. _____
5. _____

Which qualities within yourself have served as your greatest strengths throughout life's journey? What essential aspects of your character have you come to value most deeply in yourself as you've gained wisdom and perspective?"

1. _____
2. _____
3. _____
4. _____
5. _____

Whose musical voices have most consistently provided the soundtrack to your life's significant chapters? Which artists' expressions have resonated most deeply with your own emotional landscape across the years?"

1. _____
2. _____
3. _____
4. _____
5. _____

What wisdom would you whisper across time to your younger self standing at the threshold of adulthood? Which understandings, had they come earlier, might have illuminated your path or eased your journey's more challenging passages?"

1.
2.
3.
4.
5.

Which luminaries from throughout human history would you choose for an evening of conversation and connection? Whose minds or hearts call to yours across time and circumstance, promising meaningful exchange?"

1.
2.
3.
4.
5.

Which frozen delights have most consistently brought you that singular pleasure unique to ice cream? What flavors carry the sweetest associations with particular moments or seasons of your life?"

1.
2.
3.
4.
5.

How would sudden abundance reshape your choices and priorities if fortune smiled upon you with extraordinary wealth? Which dreams, long held perhaps in quieter corners of your heart, would suddenly find expression with such resources?"

1.
2.
3.
4.
5.

Which gifts have transcended mere objects to become treasured symbols of connection or turning points in your life? What offerings from others revealed a profound understanding of who you truly are or what you deeply value?

1.
2.
3.
4.
5.

Things I Love

COLOR	WEEKEND MEAL
CHILDHOOD TOY	MOVIE SNACK
BOOK	HOT DRINK
VACATION SPOT	SPORT TO WATCH
SEASON	TOOL OR GADGET
SUNDAY ROUTINE	CHILDHOOD GAME
CANDY	GO-TO COMFORT FOOD
TV SHOW	MOVIE
WAY TO RELAX	DRINK (ALCOHOLIC OR NOT)
PLACE I'VE BEEN	SOUND OR SONG

Quick Questions

Which number has taken on special significance or talismanic meaning in your personal mythology? What stories or associations have imbued this particular digit with its power in your life?

_____
_____
_____

Which atmospheric conditions most deeply resonate with your spirit or temperament? How does your preferred weather reflect aspects of your inner landscape or emotional sensibilities?

_____
_____
_____

Has the document of international passage been part of your life's journey? What stories might this official booklet tell about your relationship with borders and distant horizons?

_____
_____
_____

Which nourishment offers both physical comfort and emotional solace during times of illness? What associations between care, flavor, and healing have formed throughout your life's vulnerable moments?

_____
_____
_____

Which daily rhythm has your body and spirit most naturally embraced? How has your relationship with dawn or dusk shaped your approach to life's daily unfolding?

___

How have you engaged with games of chance and possibility throughout your life? What patterns or rituals have you created around these small investments in potential transformation?

___

Which mastery has called to you across the years, perhaps just beyond reach? What skill or knowledge, if suddenly granted, would most fulfill some long-harbored desire or curiosity?

___

What reliable sources of joy have consistently broken through life's serious moments? Which people, memories, or situations have held the power to awaken your laughter even in challenging times?

___

If the boundaries of possibility suddenly expanded through magical intervention, which deepest desires would you prioritize? What would these chosen wishes reveal about your values and unfulfilled longings?

___

Which modest joys consistently illuminate your days with meaning and contentment? What unpretentious delights have provided sustenance for your spirit throughout life's journey?

___

When has your skill, luck, or effort been recognized through formal victory? What stories of achievement, perhaps unexpected, have become part of your narrative of accomplishment?

___

On which purchase have you most dramatically departed from your usual patterns of spending? What exceptional acquisition represents a significant investment of your resources, and what prompted this departure?

___

Which journey along highways and byways stretched furthest in both distance and experience? What discoveries unfolded during this extended traverse through changing landscapes?

___

To which distant horizon has your life's journey taken you, farthest from your point of origin? How did this maximum geographical displacement influence your perspective on home and distance?

___

How has your relationship with fate, chance, and unseen influences expressed itself in small rituals or beliefs? Which patterns or practices honor the mysterious aspects of existence in your daily life?

Which recurring pattern in your behavior has proven most resistant to change? What personal tendency do you recognize as limiting, yet find yourself returning to despite your better intentions?

How does your spirit navigate the balance between careful deliberation and impulsive action? Which approach to life's unfolding possibilities has most authentically expressed your true nature?

When has your physical form experienced significant fracture or injury? What stories of resilience or vulnerability reside in the history of your body's encounters with the world's harder edges?

Which responsibilities or tasks most consistently activate your tendency to delay or postpone? What insights have you gained about the deeper reasons behind your resistance to these particular demands?

How do you understand the interplay between destiny and choice in weaving the tapestry of your life? What experiences have shaped your perspective on how much of our journey is written in advance?

___
___
___

Which expenditures strike you as fundamentally misaligned with genuine value or meaning? How has your relationship with money and worth evolved through your experiences of both abundance and limitation?

___
___
___

Which gesture of love has most deeply touched or surprised you with its thoughtfulness? What expression of romantic connection stands out as particularly meaningful in the story of your heart's journey?

___
___
___

Which words of wisdom have served as a compass through your life's various terrains? What distilled insight consistently returns to you as guidance when navigating life's complexities or challenges?

___
___
___

How do you most meaningfully mark the anniversary of your arrival in this world? Which elements transform the passage of another year into an occasion for genuine celebration or reflection?

___
___
___

Whose paths of renown or significance have intersected with your own life journey? What circumstances created these memorable crossings between your story and those whose names are more widely known?

_____
_____
_____

Which combination of place, pace, and purpose would constitute your perfect respite from everyday life? What elements must be present for you to experience true restoration and delight when away from your routine?

_____
_____
_____

What dwelling place exists in your imagination as the perfect expression of sanctuary and self? How would this ideal habitat reflect your deepest values and desires for how life might be lived?

_____
_____
_____

Which places have held your daily life within their boundaries, streets, and rhythms? What succession of cities and towns have witnessed your evolution as you've moved through different chapters of your story?

_____
_____
_____

Which destinations call to your spirit from across distances yet untraveled? If all practical constraints dissolved, what landscapes, cultures, or sacred sites would you most long to experience with your own senses?

_____
_____
_____

Words for the Ones I Love

Words for the Ones I Love

USE THIS SPACE TO SHARE A MESSAGE WITH SOMEONE YOU LOVE

Words for the Ones I Love

Words for the Ones I Love

Words for the Ones I Love

Words for the Ones I Love

www.ingramcontent.com/pod-product-compliance
Lightning Source LLC
Chambersburg PA
CBHW060413010526
44107CB00006B/673